Japan

Tom Streissguth

Carolrhoda Books, Inc. / Minneapolis

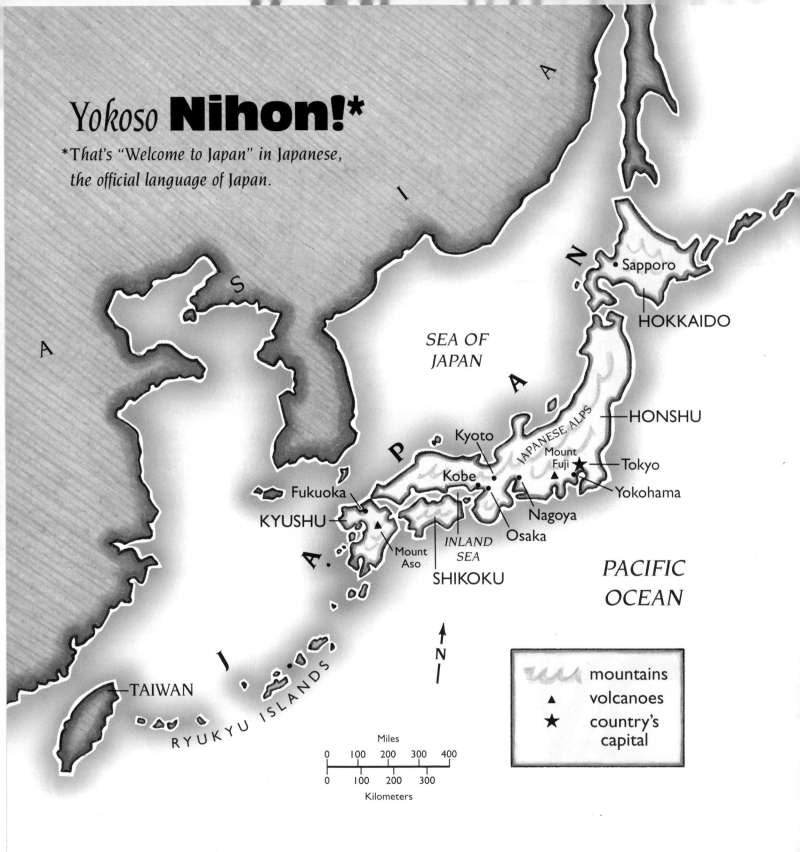

Yokoso **Nihon!***

*That's "Welcome to Japan" in Japanese,
the official language of Japan.

SEA OF
JAPAN

Sapporo

HOKKAIDO

HONSHU

JAPANESE ALPS

Kyoto

Mount
Fuji

Tokyo

Kobe

Yokohama

Fukuoka

Nagoya

KYUSHU

Osaka

Mount
Aso

INLAND
SEA

SHIKOKU

PACIFIC
OCEAN

TAIWAN

RYUKYU ISLANDS

N

	mountains
▲	volcanoes
★	country's capital

Miles

0   100   200   300   400

0   100   200   300

Kilometers

The only way to travel among Japan's 4,000 islands is by boat or by plane. You can see on the map that Japan is surrounded by water. The Pacific Ocean washes against the eastern coast. In the west, the Sea of Japan separates the country from the continent of Asia.

Japan's islands are arranged like stepping stones. They stretch for 1,700 miles. Most people live on one of the four main islands—Kyushu, Shikoku, Honshu, or Hokkaido.

The Japanese chain of islands is long and narrow. Honshu, the biggest island, is no more than 230 miles wide. That means you're never too far from a beach! From the air

Islands dot the waters of the Inland Sea.

Fast Facts about Japan

Name: Nihon or Nippon (Japan)
Area: 145,870 square miles
Main Landforms: Main islands of Honshu, Hokkaido, Kyushu, Shikoku; Ryukyu Islands; Japanese Alps; Mount Fuji; Sea of Japan
Highest Point: Fuji (12,388 feet)
Lowest Point: Sea level
Animals: Red foxes, herons, brown bears, macaques, giant salamanders
Capital City: Tokyo
Other Major Cities: Yokohama, Osaka, Nagoya, Sapporo, Kyoto, Kobe, Fukuoka
Official Language: Japanese
Money Unit: Yen

you can see that Japan is a very mountainous country. The Japanese Alps rise in central Honshu. The Ryukyu Islands are actually mountains that start on the seafloor. The mountains rise above the water's surface to form islands.

Tokyo, the capital city of Japan, is packed with buildings and people.

Many People, Little Room

Japan's steep, rocky mountains don't exactly make it easy to build a city or grow crops. So the Japanese chose to build on the flat **plains** in coastal areas. Japan's 126 million people cram themselves into these few areas. And that means crowds! Japan is one of the world's most people-packed countries. An average of 850 people live in just one square mile of Japanese territory.

Believe it or not, eight million people live in Tokyo, the capital. That means more than 35,000 people make their homes in one Tokyo square mile. That would be like 50 people living in your bedroom. Now that's crowded! Giant traffic jams stop cars and trucks. Commuters on bikes and motorcycles jostle for space. Below the city's high-rise buildings, workers and shoppers fill the sidewalks.

Cars hustle by on city streets (left). **Many Japanese towns** (above) **are built along mountainsides.**

A "Sub" Sandwich

One fast way to travel between major cities is to ride a bullet train. These trains travel at 155 miles per hour! Tickets can cost up to $130 a seat.

To travel (more slowly) within Tokyo, people can take a subway—or underground train that goes throughout the city. Passengers jam into the cars. To make sure the doors close, subway workers wearing white gloves are ready at the busiest stops. Their job is to politely shove the last few passengers into the car.

Steam rises from the crater of Mount Aso.

The Making
of Islands

Long, long ago, **volcanoes** on the ocean floor began to create the islands of Japan. These volcanoes erupted and spewed out **lava,** or melted rock. The piles of lava got so high, they peeked out of the water to form Japan. About 50 volcanoes still erupt from time to time. Mount Aso, on

A Hot Bath

All this volcanic activity heats the water that lies underground. At certain spots, hot water breaks through the surface and forms a spring. The Japanese like to visit hot springs. After cleaning themselves outside the spring, bathers then slide into the pool for a long soak. The water may be pretty hot. At some springs, workers slap the water with paddles to keep it from boiling.

Kyushu, is the most active volcano in the world. But most of Japan's 150 or so volcanoes are **dormant,** meaning they no longer erupt. Some have become beautiful snowcapped peaks.

The country's most famous dormant volcano, Fuji, is sacred to the Japanese. The highest point in Japan, Fuji last erupted in 1707. Every day people make the hard climb to the top, where a small **shrine** has been set up. Climbers can rest and take in the view of Honshu, Tokyo, and the Pacific Ocean.

If you see a name for a place in Japanese, you can sometimes guess what that place is. The Japanese often use the following word endings to name places:

Japanese ending	English meaning
-san (SAHN)	mountain
-ko (KOH)	lake
-jima (JEE-mah)	island
-wan (WAHN)	bay
-gawa (GAH-wah)	river
-taki (TAH-kee)	waterfall

What are these: Fujisan, Shinano-gawa, Iwo Jima, Otrowano-taki, Akan-ko, Kagoshima-wan?

Mount Fuji towers in the background.

Living on the Edge

Every day there's an earthquake somewhere in Japan. The ground begins to rumble. Streets shake, and people cling to trees, lampposts, and telephone poles. Overhead the telephone wires tremble. Then, suddenly, everything is still. It was just a small earthquake this time.

Tsunamis also threaten Japan. A tsunami is a giant wave that occurs when an earthquake or a volcanic eruption happens on the seafloor. Tsunamis can be tall—some are 100 feet! That's about as tall as a ten-story building. Can you imagine such a huge wall of water heading your way?

Fire is yet another danger in Japan. From time to time, fires start in old wooden homes and sweep through entire neighborhoods and

Earthquakes (top) **cause lots of destruction. Students** (left) **practice earthquake drills to help them in case of an emergency.**

cities. The Japanese are used to rebuilding their homes after such disasters. New buildings are made of concrete and steel because these materials are stronger and more flexible. If the ground shakes, the building moves, too. Wiggly buildings, you say? Well, this helps the building survive a strong earthquake. It's also much harder for a building made of concrete and steel to burn.

Too Much Waste!

Pollution— an everyday disaster in Japan. Smoke pours into the sky, and trash piles up. There's not much room for garbage dumps, so much of the country's trash goes into the sea. In recent years, though, the Japanese have become big recyclers. In fact, they use their trash problem to solve their space problem. How? By creating land where there was none before—by filling in coastal areas with garbage!

One Japanese folktale says that a giant catfish lives beneath the land. Once in a while, the catfish swings his huge tail and starts another *jishin*—or earthquake.

11

The **Japanese**

Very few non-Japanese people live in Japan. In fact, 99 out of 100 people in Japan are ethnic Japanese. Why? The story goes back about 10,000 years, when the first ancestors of the Japanese came to the islands. At that time, a narrow strip of land connected Japan to Asia. Over thousands of years, the earth warmed, and the ice near the North Pole melted. This change caused the ocean to rise and cover the land bridge. The people settled down to island life. They fished and grew rice. Few foreigners visited. Even fewer stayed.

Much later Japan closed itself off from the outside world. Japan's leaders felt they couldn't trust foreigners. These leaders didn't want different religions and ideas to

All for One!

The Japanese come from the same ancestors, speak the same language, and share the same culture. They often feel separate from the rest of the world. To succeed, they feel it is important to work together. That goes for people in a family, in school, in a business, or as a nation. Cooperation is a big part of Japanese culture. The word *wah*, meaning harmony, is often used to describe Japanese society.

If you met a Japanese friend on the street, the polite thing to do is to bow. The Japanese bow to say, "hello," "good-bye," "I'm sorry," and "thank you."

change the Japanese people. For almost 250 years, no visitors were allowed to enter. A Japanese person could be put to death for traveling overseas or for trading goods with foreigners.

When Japan opened its borders again in 1868, the country experienced a great shock. The outside world looked very different from Japan. Other nations had factories, steam-powered boats, and telegraphs. The Japanese wanted to compete. To succeed they had to master the new technologies. And their hard work soon paid off. Japan has become one of the largest makers of high-tech equipment and sends its cars to countries all over the globe.

Who Else Lives **in Japan?**

The Ainu were the first settlers of Japan. Many of them wear traditional clothes and perform ceremonies handed down by their ancestors.

The Ainu lived on the Japanese islands before other settlers arrived. When the Japanese came, most Ainu moved to the northernmost island of Hokkaido. Over the years, the Ainu have married Japanese and have had children. About 24,000 people in Japan have Ainu ancestors.

The Ainu told tales about themselves in long poems called *uwepekere*. Older Ainu would repeat these poems from memory to their children and grandchildren. But the Ainu have no written language, so they can't record and preserve their myths. Older Ainu die, and the younger Ainu are forgetting the uwepekere.

Koreans belong to the largest minority group in Japan. Other minority groups include people from China, Vietnam, Brazil, Peru, South Africa, and North America. During World War II (1939–1945), Japan forced some Koreans to come to Japan and work in Japanese factories. More Koreans have **immigrated** to Japan since then.

Many Koreans have taken Japanese names and speak Japanese. Japan does not allow Koreans to become citizens. Even if their families have lived in Japan for many years, Koreans can't vote, and most of them hold low-paying jobs.

Ho-limlim

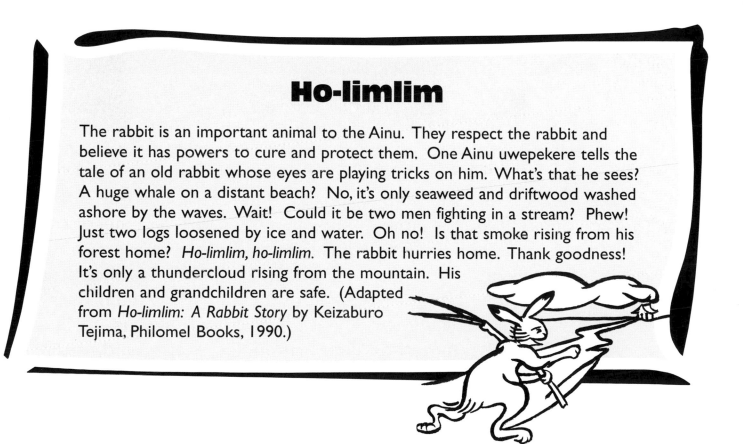

The rabbit is an important animal to the Ainu. They respect the rabbit and believe it has powers to cure and protect them. One Ainu uwepekere tells the tale of an old rabbit whose eyes are playing tricks on him. What's that he sees? A huge whale on a distant beach? No, it's only seaweed and driftwood washed ashore by the waves. Wait! Could it be two men fighting in a stream? Phew! Just two logs loosened by ice and water. Oh no! Is that smoke rising from his forest home? *Ho-limlim, ho-limlim.* The rabbit hurries home. Thank goodness! It's only a thundercloud rising from the mountain. His children and grandchildren are safe. (Adapted from *Ho-limlim: A Rabbit Story* by Keizaburo Tejima, Philomel Books, 1990.)

Japanese students enjoy talking with an American exchange student. Sometimes they use gestures to get their point across.

Gaijin **da!**

If you visited Japan, you might hear this phrase. It means, "That's a foreigner!" The Japanese use the word gaijin for anyone who is not Japanese. No matter how long a foreigner lives in Japan, he or she will always be gaijin.

Japanese people are curious about gaijin, especially in small towns where foreigners are rare. If local people spot gaijin, they may point and stare. They see gaijin as looking different and acting differently than they do.

Some foreigners come to work in Japan, rather than to travel or visit. Most of these guest workers arrive from other Asian countries, such as the Philippines, Vietnam, Malaysia, or China. They usually take jobs in factories or as servants—jobs most Japanese don't want.

Another type of foreigner is a Japanese person who has lived abroad. Japanese workers and managers go overseas for business. Some Japanese students go to foreign universities. When they return to Japan, these people often have trouble being accepted.

Body Language

Gaijin who can't speak Japanese can use other ways to communicate. The Japanese use many gestures to get the point across.

To call someone over, wave downward with one hand. To cheer for someone, raise your hands overhead and shout, *"Ganbare!"* It means, "Hurrah!" Making a circle with your fingers or arms shows that something is good. Use these gestures and see if your friends can understand.

Sliding paper screens can make a room appear bigger or smaller.

Clever **Spaces**

There's not much space for building in Japan. Cities are crowded and most homes are small. People who live alone often have only one tiny room. An entire family may live in just two or three rooms.

The Japanese have found many clever ways to save space in their homes. In the living room, there may be only one low table. In some homes, people sleep on the floor on top of futons, or soft, cotton mattresses. In the morning, the futons are folded up and stored.

In more traditional homes, thin paper screens, rather than walls, divide the rooms. The screens can be moved around to make an area bigger or smaller. A single space can be

used as a dining room, a family room, or a bedroom.

In the suburbs of big cities are many high-rise apartment buildings. In the countryside, sturdy older homes are made of wood. These traditional homes have steep roofs held up by heavy wooden pillars. The rooms inside are low and long. A small fireplace, sits in the center of the floor. But older homes in Japan are rare. Frequent earthquakes, fires, and volcanoes have destroyed most of them.

Tatami

How big is your bedroom? The Japanese measure their homes by tatami mats. These mats, made from rushes or marsh grasses, cover the floors throughout the house. The mats are about three and a half feet wide by seven feet long. An average room is four or five tatami mats. To keep the mats clean and to keep them from wearing out too quickly, the Japanese remove their shoes before entering the house.

Futons air in the sunshine.

The table is set with chopsticks and dishes for dinner.

Family **Roles**

"*Tadaima!*"

"I'm home," Japanese children shout when they arrive home. Dinner is almost ready, and a table is set with chopsticks and bowls of sauce.

In most Japanese families, the father has an office job, the mother works at home, and the children go

All in the Family

Here are the Japanese words for family members. Practice using these terms on your own family. See if they can understand you!

grandfather	*ojiisan*	(oh-JEE-ee-sahn)
grandmother	*obaasan*	(oh-BAH-ah-sahn)
father	*otosan*	(oh-TOH-sahn)
mother	*okasan*	(oh-KAH-sahn)
uncle	*ojisan*	(OH-jee-sahn)
aunt	*obasan*	(OH-bah-sahn)
son	*musuko*	(MOO-soo-koh)
daughter	*musume*	(MOO-soo-may)
brother	*onisan*	(oh-NEE-sahn)
sister	*onesan*	(oh-NAY-sahn)

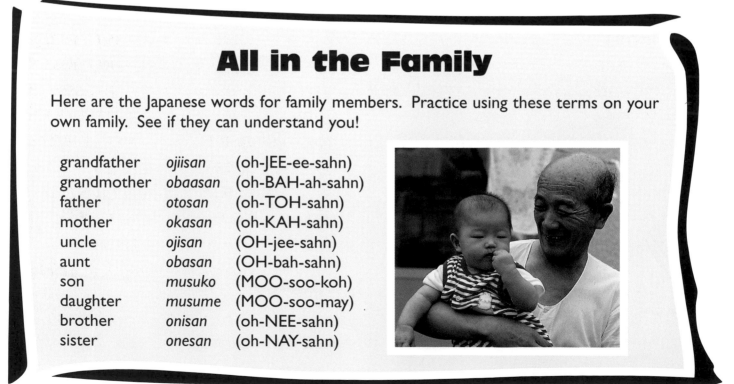

The whole family joins the birthday celebration.

to school. Japanese parents want their children to get into good universities. To make sure the kids have enough time and quiet for homework, room is set aside where the young people can study.

Japanese fathers work long hours. They often put in overtime and don't leave before the boss does. When the father gets ready to leave, he may apologize to other workers who are still at their desks.

Japanese men go out with other workers in the evenings. This is an important part of the job, too. But it also means the father may only see his family on weekends.

A few Japanese women run large companies. But after they marry, most women quit their jobs and stay home. They may use part of each day to shop for fresh food. They prepare the meals and raise the children. They also handle the family's money. Each week wives give a small allowance to their husbands for train fare and lunch. These days more Japanese women are returning to work after their youngest child has entered school.

School **Days**

It's a warm spring day in April, and the Japanese school year has just begun. At the school, a group of teachers waits for the pupils to arrive. For children going to school for the first time, the days of goofing around and speaking out of turn are over. Starting school means Japanese children begin practicing to be adults.

Every school follows a strict schedule. All over Japan, students in the same grade study the same subjects. They solve problems and memorize lots of information. Ugh! Teachers assign homework every night, and Japanese parents want their children to succeed.

In February, at the end of the school year, students take a big final

Counting in Japanese

Here is some homework for you. Try counting from 1 to 10 in Japanese.

1	ichi	(EE-chee)
2	ni	(NEE)
3	san	(SAHN)
4	shi	(SHEE)
5	go	(GOH)
6	roku	(ROH-koo)
7	shichi	(SHEE-chee)
8	hachi	(HAH-chee)
9	ku	(KOO)
10	ju	(JOO)

Before school starts, Japanese schoolchildren gather in the playground. They carry leather backpacks—black for boys, red for girls.

Meet Daisuke Tomita *(left)*. He is 12 years old and in the sixth grade. Every day Daisuke and his younger brother, Kengo, walk to elementary school together. Daisuke loves social studies, but he hates math. After a long day, he's ready for supper. After he eats, Daisuke must take a bath and do two or three hours of homework before bed.

Students in Japan shop for their school uniform *(above)*.

exam. To get into high school, they must pass this test. If they want to go to a university, they must also take a college-entrance exam. These tests are very hard. Students spend many hours studying for them.

After school is out for the day, most students go to another school called a *juku*, or cramming school. This school helps them keep up with their homework or prepare for an exam. Teachers in cramming school drill students in languages, math, and other subjects.

A Japanese **Meal**

A Japanese woman serves herself some stew with a pair of chopsticks.

"*Gohan!*" If a cook says this in Japan, it's time to eat. It means both "meal" and "rice." And rice is served at every meal. White rice is the staple of Japanese cooking. Traditional foods come to the table in several small bowls. Each diner wields a pair of chopsticks. *Click-click-click* is the sound at the dinner table. Diners

A Japanese Lunchbox

A Japanese lunchbox is called a *bento*. Often, the plastic or wooden box is packed with sushi, salad, and a cup of tea. What do you pack in your bento?

Sample This

Many Japanese restaurants have *sanpuru*, or "samples," in their windows. These are small wax or plastic figures of the food the restaurant offers. Sanpuru was introduced in the late 1800s, when Japan opened its ports to foreigners. Suddenly the Japanese were eating many different kinds of strange foods. Sanpuru showed people what they were ordering.

use the wide part of the chopsticks to bring the food to their plates. People eat with the narrow end. If you've never used chopsticks before, you might find yourself very hungry at a Japanese meal. They can be tricky to master.

Instead of toast and cereal for breakfast, a family may have soup, rice, sour pickles, and dried seaweed. Large evening meals might include soup, vegetables, or tofu (soybean curd). Yakitori is grilled chicken cooked and served on a skewer. Vegetables, fish, and meat are dipped in egg batter and are fried to make tempura.

The Japanese have always made a living from the sea, which means that fish is important. Sashimi is raw fish served with soy sauce and horseradish mustard. It might take you a while to get used to the taste of sushi, which is raw fish wrapped in vinegar-flavored rice, but the Japanese love it.

Having a Good **Time**

Have you ever gone snow skiing in the summer? The Japanese can!

Pinball for Adults

Ping-ping, clink-ping-clink, chink. These are the sounds coming from one of Japan's most happenin' hangouts—the pachinko parlor. Pachinko machines are tall, narrow, metal boxes. They look like pinball machines that stand upright. The player shoots the ball to the top of the box. If the ball falls into the right hole, the player gets more balls or a small prize.

Imagine a giant playground. Then imagine one even bigger than that...one that can hold mountains and oceans. No kidding! The Japanese have built indoor beaches and ski slopes. Inside huge, enclosed playgrounds, snowmaking machines blast snow onto ski trails. In other indoor parks, trucks pour a long strip of clean sand next to a big pool. A machine creates waves that break against the shore. Instant vacation!

But these playgrounds cost a lot of money to visit. On most weekends, families visit relatives in the country,

26

sides, while battleships shift into overdrive.

explore parks, or go shopping together. On Sundays Japanese families crowd the streets. In one corner of a park there might be a **karaoke** machine. People sing while the machine plays recorded music. A crowd gathers to watch. Of course, many kids think that playing Nintendo is also a great way to pass time.

These Japanese girls practice virtual reality target shooting.

"Oh, give me a home…where the buffalo roam…." Karaoke is a popular Japanese pastime. A machine plays recorded music, and someone from the audience supplies the voice. The words to the song appear on a small screen. The word *karaoke* means "empty orchestra." Some homes have karaoke players. Even cars have karaoke machines. Rush-hour drivers can sing while they fight through traffic. What better way to pass the time?

Home run! Kids in Japan love to play baseball every chance they get.

Sports in **Japan**

"*Puure booru!*" cries the umpire to begin the game. *Crack!* The ball flies off the bat and sails toward the left field wall.

The Japanese are crazy about *yakyu*, or baseball. A U.S. teacher introduced the sport to the Japanese in 1873. And baseball has been popular ever since. Many Japanese ball teams have taken names from

Sidetrack

The Japanese love to watch other sports, too. In 1993 the first Japanese professional soccer league made its appearance. *Sakka*, or soccer, already has many devoted fans.

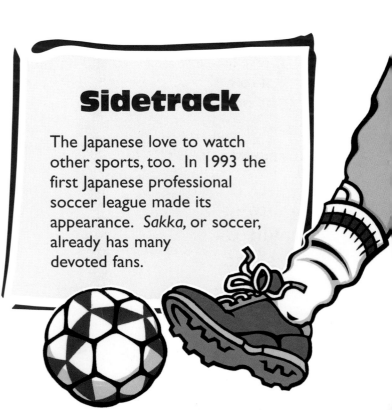

Sumo Wrestling

Grunt! Snort! Stomp! If you heard these sounds, chances are you'd either be face to face with a bull or watching the Japanese national sport of sumo wrestling. Sumo wrestling exists only in Japan. Six wrestling tournaments are held each year, and the audience is always packed.

The sumo ring is round and so is the sumo wrestler. Wrestlers often weigh more than 300 pounds. To get big, they eat *chanko*—a heavy stew made with meat, vegetables, tofu, and eggs. Wrestlers are big, but they are also very strong.

Before the match starts, the wrestlers circle one another in the ring, clapping their hands, stamping their feet, and throwing their arms in the air. Wrestlers each study how the other moves. The referee shouts to start the match. The wrestlers grunt and rush toward one another. They can use any of the 68 official sumo holds. They must stay on their feet inside the ring. If a wrestler falls to the ground or touches the ground with any other part of his body, he loses. Many matches last only a few seconds.

American sports teams, such as the Yomiuri Giants, the Kintetsu Buffaloes, and the Seibu Lions.

A baseball game in Japan is not always a tame event. Players yell at the umpire if they disagree with a call, and managers shout at players. Baseball is not just a spectator sport, either. On playgrounds you can almost always find a game in progress.

On **Stage**

A puppeteer (left) **may study for years to learn how to make the subtle movements of the puppets. Kabuki theater** (right) **has a long tradition in Japan.**

Japan has a long tradition of theater, including Bunraku, Kabuki, and Noh. Bunraku is puppet theater. The puppets are three or four feet tall and are supposed to look like real actors. The **puppeteers,** who wear black robes to hide themselves, stand right behind the stage. A singer sitting beside the stage chants the story and does the voices for all the characters.

Kabuki plays, an age-old tradition, describe Japanese history, myths, and folktales. The plays are loud, dramatic, and exciting. The characters fight with swords. They make sweeping gestures with their

34

almost empty so the audience can focus on the words and the story. Drums and flutes play in the background. Instead of makeup, the actors wear masks. To the right of the stage stands a group of eight actors chanting along with the story.

arms and bodies. At one moment in a Kabuki play, an actor strikes a dramatic pose. The audience applauds and shouts the actor's name. Kabuki sets show castles, forests, and mountains. All the performers are men. They wear colorful costumes and many layers of white makeup to show different expressions. They have the faces of demons, kings, and warriors. Male actors also play female roles.

Noh is very different from Kabuki. Noh plays are very serious stories of Japanese history. The stage is

35

Arts and Crafts

Manga is a big hit in Japan.

A popular form of art in Japan is *manga*. This word means "lighthearted pictures." A Japanese artist has written and illustrated each manga. Similar to a comic book, manga tell various kinds of stories. Every issue continues a story. Some stories are about an ordinary person dealing with strange, supernatural forces. Others are adventure stories or a drama taking place in an office. A manga may be a tale of romance or a detective story. Manga stories are printed every week. In that time, the most popular manga sell several million copies. Children in Japan like to copy the drawings. They come up with their own stories and characters.

The most famous manga artist was Osamu Tezuka. His best-known tale is *Phoenix*. He started the story in 1954 and was still drawing it when he died in 1989.

On television you can see animated versions of manga. These stories, called *anime*, are often very violent, with characters facing death at every turn. The special effects are spectacular—spurting blood, drooling monsters, fiery rocket engines. The stories could be about anything from talking cockroaches to futuristic robot warriors. The only limitation is the creator's imagination.

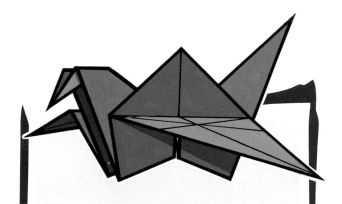

Origami

Can you imagine turning a flat piece of paper into a lion or a bird? The Japanese practice the art of origami, which is the Japanese word for "folded paper." Designs for origami run from the simple to the complex.

A traditional Japanese painting (left)—**a long-practiced art form**

37

Choosing a **Religion**

Nature is highly valued by followers of Shinto, one of Japan's main religions.

Japan has two main religions, **Buddhism** and **Shinto.** Japanese believers may follow rituals from both religions. A few Japanese also belong to Christian groups.

Buddhism came to Japan from China and Korea. Buddhists follow the ideas of the Buddha, a man who lived 2,500 years ago. Buddhist beliefs shape other areas of life. For example, Buddhists believe that happiness doesn't come from having lots of toys, a fast car, or a big house. Buddhists think that living a life of virtue and wisdom brings happiness.

Shinto is the oldest religion of Japan. The word *Shinto* means "the way of the spirits." Shintoists believe these natural spirits, or *kami*, live in trees, mountains, volcanoes, and other natural things. They are called *kamisama*. The word *sama* is used to show respect. Kamisama also include the spirits of ancestors. They demand respect. Otherwise, bad luck or problems might result.

The Tea Ceremony

From Buddhism came the *chanoyu,* or tea ceremony. This ritual is more than 500 years old. The quiet ceremony of serving and drinking tea takes place in a garden teahouse. The decorations are very simple, yet beautiful. There are certain rules and customs to follow during the chanoyu. It is a time to enjoy nature, friendship, and quiet. Many people spend years at a special school studying the proper movements of serving tea.

A *jinja* is a Shinto shrine. Visitors to the shrine pass through torii—tall wooden gates with a cross beam set high up on two posts. Visitors pass under three torii gates before entering the shrine. They ring a bell and clap three times. Inside the shrine, visitors make an offering to the kamisama. They write prayers on a small piece of paper or cloth. A student may ask for a good grade at exams. A business owner may want success for a store or restaurant.

A torii gate stands in a beautiful garden of purple azaleas.

41

Festivals and
Holidays

A *mikoshi* is a small shrine carried in parades during festivals.

New Year's Day is the first and most important holiday of the year in Japan. Before sundown on December 31, families clean their homes and decorate the fronts of their houses with pine branches. On January 1, the families visit a Shinto shrine to ask for a successful new year. Bells ring out from Buddhist temples to signal the birth of a new year. They ring 108 times—one for every sin supposed to have been committed by a person during one year—to purify the soul.

Later in the year, on March 3, Japanese girls have their own festival. People call this holiday the Festival of Dolls. Each family displays special dolls on a set of shelves. On the top shelf sit dolls of the emperor and empress of Japan. The members of the royal court stand on the lower shelves.

On May 5, Children's Day, families fly wind socks shaped like carp from a tall pole. Each fish represents a son, whom parents hope will be as healthy as the big, strong fish. The largest paper carp represents the oldest child.

The spirits of ancestors return on August 15 during the Festival of the Dead. People light paper lanterns and release them on a river or on the sea. The lanterns are said to light the way for the dead who return to the underworld.

Japan is a modern country and has a booming economy. The Japanese look to the future, but they also respect their history. Festivals are one way for Japanese to stay in touch with their past.

Matsuri

Local festivals called *matsuri* take place at different times in different cities. At the matsuri, townspeople celebrate local heroes and spirits who are a part of the town's history. The townspeople carry a small shrine called a *mikoshi*.

A crowd gathers to watch a parade during the Firefighters' Festival.

Glossary

Buddhism: A religion started in 500 B.C. based on the teachings of a religious leader called the Buddha. Followers of Buddhism believe in the cycle of life and rebirth.

character: A graphic symbol used to represent a word or letter.

dormant: Describes a volcano that no longer erupts.

ideograph: A picture symbol that illustrates a word or phrase.

immigrate: To move to another country to live.

karaoke: A machine that plays music for a variety of songs. The user sings along to words that show up on a screen.

lava: Hot, liquid rock that emerges from an erupting volcano.

A bullet train whizzes past Mount Fuji.

martial arts: Several types of combat and self-defense, such as kendo, and karate, that were developed in China, Japan, and Korea.

plain: A broad, flat area of land that has few trees or other outstanding natural features.

puppeteer: A person who stands behind, on, or below a small stage and moves the strings attached to a puppet, causing it to move.

samurai: A well-respected class of Japanese warriors who fought for emperors long ago. They followed a code of loyalty and obedience.

Shinto: The native religion of Japan. Its followers celebrate gods of natural forces and spirits they believe are found in mountains, trees, rivers, rocks, and other natural things.

shrine: A sacred place that may contain religious images.

syllable: A unit of spoken language that represents a sound grouping within a word.

tsunami: A tidal wave, which is created by undersea earthquakes or volcanic eruptions.

volcano: An opening in the earth's surface through which hot, melted rock and gases are thrown up with explosive force. Volcano can also refer to the hill or mountain of ash and rock that builds up around the opening.

Carp windsocks blow in the breeze.

Index

Ainu, 14–15
animals, 5, 15, 39
arts and crafts, 36–37
Aso, Mount, 8–9

Buddhism, 40, 41, 42
Bunraku (puppet theater),
  34

earthquakes, 10, 11, 19
ethnic groups, 14–15

families, 20–21
festivals, 42–43
fires, 10–11, 19
food, 21, 24–25
foreigners, 12–13, 16–17
Fuji, Mount, 5, 9

gaijin, 16–17
games, 26–27

Hokkaido, 5, 14
holidays, 42–43
homes, 6, 18–19
Honshu, 5, 9
hot springs, 8

Japlish, 33
jobs, 17, 20, 21

Kabuki plays, 34–35
kana, 32–33
kanji, 32, 33
karate, 30, 31
Koreans, 15
Kyushu, 5, 9

language, 5, 9, 20, 22, 32–33

manga, 36–37
map of Japan, 4
martial arts, 30–31
mountains, 5, 6
music, 27, 38–39

Noh plays, 35

origami, 37

people, 12–13
pollution, 11
population, 6
puppeteers, 34

religion, 40–41
Ryukyu Islands, 5

schools, 16, 17, 21, 22–23
Sea of Japan, 5
Shikoku, 5

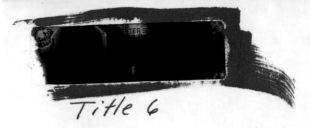